Chicago   New York
Dallas   Philadelphia
Detroit   Phoenix
Houston   San Antonio
Los Angeles   San Diego

AMERICA'S TOP 10 CITIES

By
Jenny Tesar

Published by Blackbirch Press, Inc.
260 Amity Road
Woodbridge, CT 06525

©1998 Blackbirch Press, Inc.
First Edition

Printed in the USA

10 9 8 7 6 5 4 3 2 1

Library of Congress Cataloging-in-Publication Data

Tesar, Jenny E.
    America's top 10 cities / by Jenny Tesar.
        p. cm.—(America's top 10)
    Includes bibliographical references and index.
    Summary: Presents information and statistics about the ten most populated cities in
the United States: New York, Los Angeles, Chicago, Houston, Philadelphia, San Diego,
Phoenix, Dallas, San Antonio, and Detroit.
    ISBN 1-56711-191-2 (lib. bdg. : alk. paper)
    1. Cities and towns—United States—Growth—Juvenile literature. 2. Metropolitan
areas—United States—Juvenile literature. I. Title. II. Series.
HT123.T437 1998   96–51581
307.76'0973—dc21   CIP
                                                                  AC

BLACKBIRCH PRESS, INC.
WOODBRIDGE, CONNECTICUT

AMERICA'S TOP

10

CITIES

Chicago

★ ★ ★ ★ ★ ★ ★ ★ ★ ★ ★ ★ ★ ★ ★ ★ ★ ★ ★ ★

Chicago is located on the southwestern shore of Lake Michigan. It is the only inland city in the country that is connected by water to both the Atlantic Ocean and the Gulf of Mexico. Chicago's location has made it an important transportation center since the early 1800s. Many highways and railroad routes meet in Chicago, and it has 3 airports—including O'Hare International Airport, the busiest airport in the world. The city was founded by Jean Baptiste Point du Sable, a fur trader, in 1779.

Chicago is famous for its spectacular architecture. The world's first skyscraper, the Home Insurance Company, was built there in 1885. It was 9 stories tall. Today, 3 of the world's 10 tallest buildings are in Chicago: the Sears Tower (the tallest building in America), the Amoco Building, and the John Hancock Center.

The central business area is called the Loop. Originally, this area was within a loop of elevated train tracks. North of the Loop is the Chicago River. Its flow was reversed by engineers in 1900 to prevent industrial wastes from flowing into Lake Michigan. It is the only river in the world that flows backward! Every year on St. Patrick's Day, the Chicago River is dyed green.

For much of the last century, Chicago has been known for its stockyards and meat-processing plants, and today, food processing is still a leading industry. For example, Chicago is home to the Nabisco Biscuit Company, the world's largest cookie and cracker factory, where 16 billion Oreo cookies are made each year.

Name: From the Potawatomi name, Checaugou, meaning "place of the wild onion"
Nickname: Windy City
Location: Illinois
Incorporated: 1837
Population and rank: 2.7 million; 3rd largest
Size: 228 square miles
Elevation: 623 feet
Important industries: Financial services, food processing, manufacturing, transportation, wholesale and retail trade
Landmarks: Amoco Building, Buckingham Fountain, John Hancock Center, Sears Tower
Tallest building: Sears Tower (110 stories)
Sports teams: Cubs, White Sox (baseball); Bears (football); Bulls (basketball); BlackHawks (hockey)
Fun fact: The first zippers were made here in 1896.

Opposite page:
Chicago is home to 3 of the world's tallest buildings, including the John Hancock Center (black building).

AMERICA'S TOP
10
CITIES

Dallas

★ ★ ★ ★ ★ ★ ★ ★ ★ ★ ★ ★ ★ ★ ★ ★ ★ ★ ★

Dallas is an important manufacturing center. Airplane parts, electronic equipment, processed foods, machinery, and clothing are all made there. The city also is a major financial and commercial center. Each year, hundreds of thousands of people go to Dallas to buy merchandise for their stores and businesses. Most of them arrive by plane, landing at DFW International Airport, the world's third-busiest airport. DFW takes up more space than New York's island of Manhattan!

The city was founded in 1841, when John Neely Bryan opened a trading post on the banks of the Trinity River. Bryan sketched out a town, including a courthouse square and 20 streets. Settlers came, and gradually the city grew. Today, it is America's eighth-largest city, filled with tall, modern buildings. Dallas's past is still remembered, however. In Historical Plaza is the small log cabin built by Bryan more than 150 years ago. Nearby, in Pioneer Plaza, is a sculpture of larger-than-life bronze longhorn steers and cowboys on horseback. These figures are located on an actual cattle trail that was used in the 1800s.

One of the city's most popular events is the state fair, held each fall. The largest state fair in America, it opens with a parade downtown. Most of the activities take place in Fair Park, where many of the buildings date back to the Texas Centennial Exposition—the 6-month 100th birthday party for the state. These buildings form the oldest world's fair site in the United States. Another park landmark is Cotton Bowl Stadium, where football games and other events are held.

Name: There are several explanations. The name may honor George Mifflin Dallas, vice president of the United States in 1846.

Nickname: Big D

Location: Texas

Incorporated: 1856

Population and rank: 1 million; 8th largest

Size: 378 square miles

Elevation: 450 to 750 feet

Important industries: Commerce, finance, manufacturing, transportation

Landmarks: Fair Park, Historical Plaza, Pioneer Plaza

Tallest building: NationsBank (72 stories)

Sports teams: Rangers (baseball), Cowboys (football), Mavericks (basketball), Stars (hockey), Sidekicks (indoor soccer)

Fun fact: The Tex-Mex dish chicken fajitas was invented here.

Opposite page:
The modern Dallas skyline mixes with the city's pioneer past.

AMERICA'S TOP
10
CITIES

Detroit

Detroit is often called Motor City—or Motown, for short. Henry Ford began his Ford Motor Company in Detroit in 1903. Soon, Walter Chrysler and Ransom Olds also built automobile plants there. Since that time, the city has been the center of America's automotive industry. About 20 percent of the nation's cars, trucks, and tractors are manufactured in Detroit and the surrounding towns. The city is also home to the world's largest market for small, flowering garden plants.

Detroit was founded in 1701 by a Frenchman named Antoine de la Mothe Cadillac. He established a fur trading post on the west bank of what became known as the Detroit River. The trading post grew into Detroit, America's 10th largest city.

Soaring high into the sky in downtown Detroit is the Renaissance Center. This building complex has 6 office towers, a hotel, and dozens of stores and restaurants. An elevated train, known as the People Mover, connects downtown sites.

Among Detroit's tourist attractions are mansions that automakers built. Meadow Brook Hall was built by John Dodge in the late 1920s. It has 100 rooms and 39 brick chimneys. On the grounds is Knole Cottage, with miniature rooms two-thirds normal size. It was built for Dodge's 12-year-old daughter and was the first all-electric home in Detroit!

Belle Isle, an island in the city, is a popular park for picnics, fishing, baseball, and racquetball. The nation's oldest freshwater aquarium is also located there.

Name: From French words meaning "the straits"
Nicknames: Motor City, Motown, Motor Capital of the World
Location: Michigan
Incorporated: 1802
Population and rank: 992,038; 10th largest
Size: 137 square miles
Elevation: 600 feet
Important industries: Automobile manufacturing and trade, shipping
Landmarks: Belle Isle, Meadow Brook Hall, Renaissance Center
Tallest building: Westin Hotel (73 stories)
Sports teams: Tigers (baseball), Lions (football), Pistons (basketball), Red Wings (hockey)
Fun fact: The world's first concrete road was built here.

Opposite page:
The lights of downtown Detroit glisten along the Detroit River.

AMERICA'S TOP

10

CITIES

Houston

★ ★ ★ ★ ★ ★ ★ ★ ★ ★ ★ ★ ★ ★ ★ ★

Houston is the largest city in Texas. It is one of the nation's busiest ports and is the center of America's petroleum industry. Houston is also known for its aerospace industry. The Johnson Space Center designs space missions, trains astronauts, and acts as mission control during flights. At the Space Center, visitors of all ages can direct a space shuttle and space station.

Houston was founded in 1836 by Augustus and John Allen. After sailing up from the Gulf of Mexico, the explorers hired Gail Borden—the inventor of condensed milk—to create a map for the city. The Allens named it after General Samuel Houston, who earlier that year led the Texas army to victory over Mexican forces, gaining independence for Texas.

Some of the city's original buildings still stand, including Kennedy Bakery, built in 1861. In addition to being a bakery, this building also served as an arsenal and a trading post. In Sam Houston Park, the San Jacinto Monument marks the victorious battle for Texas independence.

In the early 1900s, the Houston Ship Channel was created. This 50-mile-long waterway made it possible for large ocean-going ships to travel between Houston and the Gulf of Mexico.

Twenty feet below Houston's downtown is the nation's largest tunnel system. Located in the 6 miles of tunnels are shops and more than 100 restaurants. Just outside the downtown area is the world-famous Astrodome, the world's first domed stadium. It is home to several professional sports teams and the world's largest rodeo.

Name: Honors Samuel Houston, a hero of the Texas war for independence from Mexico

Nicknames: Space City, Bayou City

Location: Texas

Incorporated: 1836

Population and rank: 1.7 million; 4th largest

Size: 573 square miles

Elevation: 49 feet

Important industries: Aerospace, biotechnology, chemicals, oil refining, shipping

Landmarks: Astrodome, Hermann Park, Johnson Space Center, San Jacinto Monument

Tallest building: Transco Tower (64 stories)

Sports teams: Astros (baseball), Oilers (football), Rockets (basketball), Aeros (hockey), Hotshots (indoor soccer)

Fun fact: Home of the world's first domed stadium

Opposite page:
Underneath Houston's skyscrapers lies America's largest tunnel system.

AMERICA'S TOP

10

CITIES

Los Angeles

Often called by its initials—L.A.—Los Angeles is located in sunny southern California. Hollywood, which is part of L.A., has made the city America's entertainment capital. It is a famous center for the motion picture, television, radio, and music-recording industries.

Los Angeles is bordered by the Pacific Ocean to the west and south. To the north and east are mountains. The city was established in 1781, when 44 settlers from Mexico made their homes in what is now the downtown area. It remained a small community until the gold rush of 1849, which brought more settlers. Today, Los Angeles is America's second-largest city. Because it is spread out over a large area, almost everyone travels by car. The city is famous for its system of 6- and 8-lane freeways, or highways.

The city's government and financial centers are located downtown. There, too, are ethnic communities such as Chinatown and Little Tokyo. In Hancock Park are the famous La Brea Tar Pits. Thousands of years ago, oil seeped up from deep within the ground, forming pools on the surface. Animals became trapped in the sticky pools and died. The remains of these animals tell us that camels, mastodons, and saber-tooth tigers once lived in southern California.

Hollywood is north of downtown L.A. Along its sidewalks is the Walk of Fame, where colorful stones display the names of celebrities. Hand-prints and footprints of movie stars are embedded in cement in the famous courtyard of Mann's Chinese Theater (a movie theater).

Name: Originally El Pueblo de Nuestra Señora de los Angeles de Porciuncula ("The Village of Our Lady of the Angels")
Nicknames: L.A., City of Angels
Location: California
Incorporated: 1781
Population and rank: 3.5 million; 2nd largest
Size: 467 square miles
Elevation: 104 feet
Important industries: Health services, international trade, motion pictures, television, tourism
Landmarks: Hollywood Walk of Fame, La Brea Tar Pits
Tallest building: First Interstate World Center (73 stories)
Sports teams: Dodgers (baseball), Clippers, Lakers (basketball), Kings (hockey)
Fun fact: More than 100 tons of fossilized animal bones have been unearthed from La Brea Tar Pits.

Opposite page:
Los Angeles is the center of America's entertainment industry.

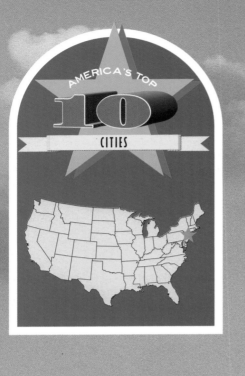

AMERICA'S TOP

10

CITIES

★ ★ ★ ★ ★ ★ ★ ★ ★ ★ ★ ★ ★ ★ ★ ★ ★ ★ ★

New York

Popularly known as "the Big Apple," New York is America's largest city. More than 7 million people live there. Each year, the city attracts more than 30 million visitors from all over the globe. Many enjoy Broadway theater productions, visit art museums and galleries, or attend music or dance concerts. The city is considered to be one of the cultural centers of the world.

New York is located on the mouth of the Hudson River, where the river flows into the Atlantic Ocean. The city is divided into 5 counties, called boroughs. Only the Bronx is on the mainland. Staten Island and Manhattan are islands. Brooklyn and Queens are part of Long Island.

Manhattan is the smallest borough, but it is the best known. It is home to many famous buildings, including the Empire State Building, World Trade Center, and United Nations headquarters, where many nations have offices.

The city is filled with well-known landmarks. On a small island in the harbor is the Statue of Liberty, a gift from France to celebrate America's first 100 years of independence. Near the statue is Ellis Island, where millions of immigrants first entered the United States.

New York was America's first capital. A statue of George Washington in front of Federal Hall marks the spot where, in 1789, Washington took the oath of office as the first president of the United States. The hall is in lower Manhattan. At the northern end of the borough is Dyckman House, built around 1783. It is the only remaining farmhouse in Manhattan.

Name: Honors England's Duke of York, who later became King James II of England
Nickname: The Big Apple
Location: New York
Incorporated: 1625, as New Amsterdam
Population and rank: 7.3 million; largest
Size: 301 square miles
Elevation: Sea level to 409 feet
Important industries: Advertising, banking, fashion, financial services, publishing
Landmarks: Central Park, Empire State Building, Statue of Liberty, United Nations, World Trade Center
Tallest buildings: World Trade Towers (110 stories)
Sports teams: Mets, Yankees (baseball), Giants, Jets (football), Knicks (basketball), Islanders, Rangers (hockey)
Fun fact: The hot dog was invented here in 1900.

Opposite page:
The Manhattan skyline rises high above the East River.

AMERICA'S TOP
10
CITIES

Philadelphia

★ ★ ★ ★ ★ ★ ★ ★ ★ ★ ★ ★ ★ ★ ★ ★ ★ ★

Located between the Delaware and Schuylkill Rivers in southeastern Pennsylvania, Philadelphia is one of the largest cities on the East Coast. The city was founded in 1682 by William Penn, an English Quaker who wanted it to be a center of religious freedom. During Colonial days, it was America's largest city. From 1790 to 1800 it was also the nation's capital.

Philadelphia is brimming with historic sites. At Independence National Historical Park is Independence Hall, where America's founders adopted the Declaration of Independence on July 4, 1776. The Liberty Bell, which was rung when the declaration was approved, is nearby. So is Carpenters Hall, where the First Continental Congress met in 1774. Today, visitors to the City Tavern can sit in the same spot where George Washington, Benjamin Franklin, and other Colonial leaders sat more than 200 years ago!

Philadelphia's first commercial area, near the waterfront, is known as Old City. The Betsy Ross House is there. According to legend, this is where Ross created the first American flag.

Along the Delaware River is a park called Penn's Landing. Historic ships, including the U.S.S. *Olympia* from the Spanish-American War, are docked there, and numerous festivals are held in the park. Philadelphia's port has been important since Colonial days. Each year, millions of tons of cargo flow through its facilities.

On the city's west side is Fairmount Park. It has more than 8,900 acres of meadows, trails, winding creeks, and the Philadelphia Zoo.

Name: Philadelphia comes from the Greek words for "brotherly love."

Nicknames: Philly, City of Brotherly Love

Location: Pennsylvania

Incorporated: 1682

Population and rank: 1.5 million; 5th largest

Size: 129 square miles

Elevation: 5 to 150 feet

Important industries: Health care, oil refining, petroleum products, pharmaceuticals, shipping

Landmarks: Fairmount Park, Independence Hall, Liberty Bell, Old City

Tallest building: Liberty Place (61 stories)

Sports teams: Phillies (baseball), Eagles (football), 76ers (basketball), Flyers (hockey)

Fun fact: The nation's first daily newspaper was published here.

Opposite page:
Philadelphia's skyline is a mix of old and new.

AMERICA'S TOP
10
CITIES

Phoenix

★ ★ ★ ★ ★ ★ ★ ★ ★ ★ ★ ★ ★ ★ ★ ★ ★ ★ ★ ★

Phoenix, the capital of Arizona, is the state's largest city. Because of its dry, sunny climate, Phoenix is a major resort center. It is also known for its high-tech and aerospace industries.

Phoenix is located along the banks of the Salt River, in the Valley of the Sun. This valley is the northern tip of the Sonoran Desert and is bordered by dramatic mountain ranges.

Many centuries ago, Native Americans known as the Hohokams lived there. They built canals from the Salt River to water their fields. For unknown reasons, the Hohokams disappeared around the year 1450. In 1865, the U.S. Army established a fort in the nearby mountains. In 1870, Phoenix was created along the lines of the ancient Hohokam canals. It had only 300 inhabitants but grew steadily. Today, many people move to Phoenix for the pleasant climate.

The city's best-known landmark is Camelback Mountain, named for its camel-like profile. Another landmark is Tovrea Castle, which was built by a wealthy cattle rancher.

South Mountain Park—the world's largest city park—covers more than 20,000 acres. More than 300 kinds of plants live there, as well as coyotes, foxes, rabbits, lizards, and many other animals. A short distance to the north of the park is the Desert Botanical Garden, which displays one of the world's best collections of desert plants.

The state capitol building was built in 1900. It was made from local materials, including stone quarried from Camelback Mountain and copper from Arizona's famous copper mines.

Name: Refers to the mythical bird that rose from its own ashes, just as the city grew from the ruins of the Hohokam civilization.
Nickname: Valley of the Sun
Location: Arizona
Incorporated: 1881
Population and rank: 1 million; 7th largest
Size: 450 square miles
Elevation: 1,117 feet
Important industries: Aerospace, construction, high-tech industry, tourism
Landmarks: Camelback Mountain, Heritage Square, South Mountain Park, Tovrea Castle
Tallest building: Bank One Building (40 stories)
Sports teams: Cardinals (football), Suns (basketball), Coyotes (hockey)
Fun fact: The Phoenix Zoo is credited with saving the Arabian oryx—a type of antelope—from extinction.

Opposite page:
Phoenix is the largest city in Arizona.

AMERICA'S TOP
10
CITIES

San Antonio

San Antonio is one of America's largest cities, and an important commercial and industrial center. The city's beginning dates back to 1691, when a group of Spanish explorers came upon a river in south-central Texas. It was the feast day of Saint Anthony, so they named the river San Antonio in his honor. In 1718, Spaniards founded a military post on the banks of the river. They also established a mission (church and fort) nearby called the Alamo. The fort became famous in 1836. For 13 days, 189 Texans held the fort against some 4,000 Mexican troops. The Texans lost the battle, but "Remember the Alamo!" became the motto of the Texas war for independence.

The Alamo and 4 other Spanish missions built in the early 1700s are among the many historic structures in the city that have been lovingly preserved. The Spanish Governor's Palace was built in 1749. Across the street is Navarro House, the home of one of the leaders of the Texas Revolution. These historic sites are museums that provide glimpses of what life was like long ago.

Some of San Antonio's old buildings have been put to new uses. One from the 1850s is the city's Cowboy Museum. Others are found in Market Square—the largest Mexican marketplace outside of Mexico.

The San Antonio River still winds through the center of the city. Along its banks is the popular Paseo del Rio, better known as River Walk. Every year, the Fiesta River Parade and the Holiday River Parade float down the river on barges.

Name: Honors the Catholic saint, San Antonio de Padua (St. Anthony of Padua)
Nicknames: Alamo City, Cradle of Texas Liberty
Location: Texas
Incorporated: 1837
Population and rank: 998,905; 9th largest
Size: 377 square miles
Elevation: 701 feet
Important industries: Medical, retail trade, tourism, wholesale
Landmarks: Alamo, River Walk, Spanish Governor's Palace, Spanish missions
Tallest building: Tower of the Americas (59 stories)
Sports teams: Spurs (basketball), Iguanas (hockey)
Fun fact: The first canned chili con carne and tamales were produced here in 1911.

Opposite page:
Among San Antonio's modern skyscrapers lie many historic buildings.

AMERICA'S TOP
10
CITIES

San Diego

San Diego lies on the Pacific Ocean in the southwest corner of California, close to the Mexican border. It is an important center of trade for the southwestern United States and for northern Mexico. It also is an important manufacturing center, particularly for the aerospace and electronics industries. A large sport-fishing fleet and a U.S. Navy base are located there as well.

San Diego is known as the birthplace of California. In 1542, explorer Juan Rodriguez Cabrillo became the first European to discover California. He sailed north from Mexico and landed in what is now San Diego Bay. In 1769, Spanish missionaries founded Mission San Diego de Alcala with the hope of converting Native Americans to Christianity. It was the first mission in California. During the same period of time, the Spanish established a base there for exploring California. This base slowly grew into one of America's largest cities. Much of the original settlement can still be seen in Old Town, and there are historic buildings in the Gaslamp Quarter, too. The quarter is surrounded by modern skyscrapers with mirror-like exteriors that appear silver, bronze, or black.

The city's most famous and most popular attraction is the San Diego Zoo, which is home to more than 3,900 animals. Many of the animals are housed in beautifully constructed natural habitats, such as Hippo Beach, Polar Bear Plunge, and Tiger River. There is also a petting zoo, a baby animal nursery, and large enclosures filled with colorful birds.

Name: Honors San Diego de Alcala de Henares (St. James of Alcala)
Nickname: Birthplace of California
Location: California
Incorporated: 1850
Population and rank: 1.2 million; 6th largest
Size: 320 square miles
Elevation: Sea level to 1,591 feet
Important industries: Electronics, government, high-tech, tourism
Landmarks: Cabrillo National Monument, Old Town, San Diego Zoo
Tallest building: Hyatt Regency San Diego (40 stories)
Sports teams: Padres (baseball), Chargers (football), Sockers (indoor soccer)
Fun fact: The first drive-through restaurant, a Jack-in-the-Box, opened here in 1951.

Opposite page:
San Diego's skyline sparkles against the deep blue Pacific Ocean.

America's Top 10 Cities are not necessarily the "best" cities, but they have the largest populations, according to 1994 U.S. Census figures. Below is a list of the capitals and the largest cities in each state.

America's Capitals and Largest Cities

State, Capital,
Largest City, Population

Alabama, Montgomery,
Birmingham, 264,527
Alaska, Juneau,
Anchorage, 253,649
Arizona, Phoenix,
Phoenix, 1,048,949
Arkansas, Little Rock,
Little Rock, 178,136
California, Sacramento,
Los Angeles, 3,448,613
Colorado, Denver,
Denver, 493,559
Connecticut, Hartford,
Bridgeport, 132,919
Delaware, Dover,
Wilmington, 72,799
Florida, Tallahassee,
Jacksonville, 665,070
Georgia, Atlanta,
Atlanta, 396,052
Hawaii, Honolulu,
Honolulu, 385,881
Idaho, Boise,
Boise, 145,987
Illinois, Springfield,
Chicago, 2,731,743
Indiana, Indianapolis,
Indianapolis, 752,279
Iowa, Des Moines,
Des Moines, 193,965
Kansas, Topeka,
Wichita, 310,236

Kentucky, Frankfort,
Louisville, 270,308
Louisiana, Baton Rouge,
New Orleans, 484,149
Maine, Augusta,
Portland, 61,982
Maryland, Annapolis,
Baltimore, 702,979
Massachusetts, Boston,
Boston, 547,725
Michigan, Lansing,
Detroit, 992,038
Minnesota, St. Paul,
Minneapolis, 354,590
Mississippi, Jackson,
Jackson, 193,097
Missouri, Jefferson City,
Kansas City, 443,878
Montana, Helena,
Billings, 86,578
Nebraska, Lincoln,
Omaha, 345,033
Nevada, Carson City,
Las Vegas, 327,878
New Hampshire, Concord,
Manchester, 96,640
New Jersey, Trenton,
Newark, 258,751
New Mexico, Santa Fe,
Albuquerque, 411,994
New York, Albany,
New York City, 7,333,253
North Carolina, Raleigh,
Charlotte, 437,797

North Dakota, Bismarck,
Fargo, 79,715
Ohio, Columbus,
Columbus, 635,913
Oklahoma, Oklahoma City,
Oklahoma City, 463,201
Oregon, Salem,
Portland, 450,777
Pennsylvania, Harrisburg,
Philadelphia, 1,524,249
Rhode Island, Providence,
Providence, 150,639
South Carolina, Columbia,
Columbia, 104,101
South Dakota, Pierre,
Sioux Falls, 109,174
Tennessee, Nashville,
Memphis, 614,289
Texas, Austin,
Houston, 1,702,086
Utah, Salt Lake City,
Salt Lake City, 171,849
Vermont, Montpelier,
Burlington, 38,306
Virginia, Richmond,
Virginia Beach, 430,295
Washington, Olympia,
Seattle, 520,947
West Virginia, Charleston,
Charleston, 56,553
Wisconsin, Madison,
Milwaukee, 617,044
Wyoming, Cheyenne,
Cheyenne, 53,559

Glossary

aerospace The study and industry of flight/aviation.
bank The land along the edge of a river or other body of water.
Colonial days The time before the American Revolution, when America was a British colony.
dredge Deepen, widen, or clean a body of water using a machine called a dredge.
elevation Distance above sea level.
ethnic A national, racial, religious, or cultural group—for example, Chinese-Americans.
freeway A high-speed road with several lanes and no intersections or stoplights.

mission A church building or community used to help spread Christianity.

skyscraper A very tall building.

stockyard A large, enclosed area where cattle or other animals are kept until they are slaughtered or shipped to other areas.

trading post A store in an area with few people, where goods are often traded rather than sold. For example, a trader may exchange clothing or blankets for a bushel of corn.

Further Reading

Aylesworth, Thomas and Virginia Aylesworth *Chicago: Hub of the Midwest*. Woodbridge, CT: Blackbirch Press, 1990.

Balcer, Bernadete and Fran O'Bryne-Pelham. *Philadelphia*. Morristown, NJ: Silver Burdett, 1988.

Bredeson, Carmen. *The Battle of the Alamo: The Fight for Texas Territory*. Brookfield, CT: Millbrook Press, 1996.

Doherty, Craig A. and Katherine M. Doherty. *The Houston Astrodome*. Woodbridge, CT: Blackbirch Press, 1996.

———. *The Sears Tower*. Woodbridge, CT: Blackbirch Press, 1995.

———. *The Statue of Liberty*. Woodbridge, CT: Blackbirch Press, 1996.

Fein, Art. *L.A. Musical Tour: A Guide to the Rock and Roll Landmarks of Los Angeles*. Winchester, MA: Faber and Faber, 1991.

Glassman, Bruce. *New York: Gateway to the New World*. Woodbridge, CT: Blackbirch Press, 1991.

Lee, Sally. *San Antonio*. Morristown, NJ: Silver Burdett, 1992.

Luhrs, Ruth J. *Kidding Around San Diego: A Young Person's Guide to the City*. Santa Fe, NM: John Muir Publications, 1991.

Moeser, June. *Four Sentinels: The Story of San Diego's Lighthouses*. San Diego, CA: Tecolote Press, 1991.

Riley, Edward M. *Starting America: The Story of Independence Hall*. Gettysburg, PA: Thomas Publications, 1990.

Stewart, G. *Houston*. Vero Beach, FL: Rourke, 1989.

———. *Los Angeles*. Vero Beach, FL: Rourke, 1989.

Zelver, Patricia. *The Wonderful Towers of Watts*. New York: Morrow, 1994.

Zimmerman, Chanda K. *Detroit*. Morristown, NJ: Silver Burdett, 1989.

Where to Get On-Line Information

Chicago	http://www.ci.chi.il.us
Dallas	http://cityview.com/dallas
Detroit	http://www.visitdetroit.com
Houston	http://www.houston/guide.com
Los Angeles	http://www.LAtimes.com/home/destla/
New York	http://www.nycvisit.com
Philadelphia	http://www.libertynet.org/phila-visitor
Phoenix	http://www.arizonaguide.phxcvb.com
San Antonio	http://www.Sanantoniocvb.com/
San Diego	http://www.sandiego.org

Index

Photo Credits

Cover and pages 2, 8, 14, 18: PhotoDisc, Inc.; cover and page 4: Courtesy of the Dallas Convention and Visitors Bureau; cover and page 6: Vito Palmisano/Courtesy of the Michigan Travel Bureau; cover and page 10: Courtesy of the Los Angeles Convention and Visitors Bureau/©1991 Michele and Tom Grimm; cover and page 12: ©Blackbirch Press, Inc.; cover and page 16: ©John Clare du Bois/Photo Researchers, Inc.; cover and page 20: ©George Schaub/Leo de Wys, Inc.